AND/OR

Jenn Marie Nunes

SWITCHBACK BOOKS
CHICAGO

Copyright © 2015 Jenn Marie Nunes. All rights reserved.

No part of this book may be reproduced without the permission of the publisher.

ISBN-13: 978-0-9861876-0-5
ISBN-10: 0986187607

Library of Congress Control Number: 2015933489

Book design: Elle Collins
Cover art: "Breath" by Kathleen Hawkes

Switchback Books
Hanna Andrews, Founding Editor
S. Whitney Holmes, Executive Director and Editor
Colleen O'Connor, Managing Editor
editors@switchbackbooks.com
www.switchbackbooks.com

TABLE OF CONTENTS

DEFINITION THE BODY — 1

CLEANLINESS IS NEXT — 13

THE SCORES ARE CURVED — 23

SITUATION (ELLE) — 33

WILL THE LANGUAGE — 37

DOPPELGANGER(S) — 49

WHEN YOU LEARN SOMETHING IT BECOMES A PART OF YOUR BODY — 61

HOW TO SET — 63

CONTINUE (UM) — 71

(EPILOGUE) THE GOOD GUIDE — 81

DEFINITION THE BODY

The topic is lovemaking. Say hand-held rose petals eye-
held slow   sweet   ness & clean

> *(The idea that lovemaking is one
> thing[1]. Every woman is someone's
> daughter he reminds*

I say sex[2]: the genitals. Especially external

> *(I like it doggy-style. Can we not talk
> about any mother   ing*

Somewhere intercourse[3]. Somewhere intercourse
incomplete. In that case intercourse[4]

---

1. -y
2. Subtopic or dialect of
3. Communication or exchanges between people or groups, especially conversation or social interaction
4. Sex

(We are full of landscapes: the pastel ocean mountain on fire at dusk the fir trees

Look into iPhones. Thumbs helpless mark. How to re late[5]

---

5. or "twaddle"

Orchestrating quality time
face down[6] in the backseat of an old cop car or say
a pounding

                      (Satin sheets catch[7]

Of belonging to my own hands
I touch yr eyelids & princess all over

                      (these Polack knuckles

My thighs sluck the vinyl. I poked my finger in each
metal ring until it stuck. The topic is who   buttered it
out

---

6. As soft inner feathers

7. To capture an animal or criminal

                                        (A word for something so ugly it

     Smoothed plastic fingers *(Electricity the purest form*
                                              texture between

Any systematically organized body of knowledge about a specific subject

                                        (A better word for something so ugly it

There are things I take into my body to whole me. There are things I take into my body to stir me. There are things I take into my body to whole them. This is where it gets political. There are things I take into my body. What have you done lately

                                          (Business doesn't get me down
                                          business gets me

If you can't beat

                                          (off

it love
making[8]

---

8. That causes somebody's success or progress

There are certain arguments that will never be won. If you believe in God. It is written. There are things I take into my body to fuck

(Birth. Control

If men got pregnant we wouldn't

(this discourse[9]

Bleeding hard plastic in my paper robe. Weak metaphor the proud flag clinic. Tiny flush the world aglow. Male of
human select
ing. Mushroom cloud. The distance from thumb to thumb.
Our written language[10]

---

9. To think logically regarded as a basis for knowledge, as distinctive from emotion, experience or
10. To change one form of energy to an author

Words make sense. I say the words making
     : the absolute truth & so transcendence lives there   not biology not breeding in the house of love

making

virtual intercourse.[11] Plastic
skin-colored mounts

> *(Note there is no breeding when girls kiss girls boys kiss boys. Dear God! she & her girlfriend are by this definition*

Around the same time married for love[12]. Try comparing it to something more concrete

> *(I wanna choke you she says. But I want you to choke me I say. We look into each other's eyes. We look into each other's eyes she ties my wrists with white twine*

---

11. In other words, the impression that the storage capacity created by the back-and-forth between the two bodies is greater than it actually is

12. A score of zero

This time the box is <3 shaped. Inside the box a mass of bloody

> *(What is the difference between crimson[13] &*

red tissue. It is about the size of yr fist. We are told to carry the box with us everywhere we go. Sometimes it is a different color but every box is read

> *(I don't work for the law the law words for*

The box is <3 shaped. We carry the box everywhere we go. Inside the <3 is a fist. Inside the fist is a box. It is full of synonyms

> *(Febreze*

It is <3 shaped w/ pink ribbon. This is taxonomy

---

13. Poetic; profound; deep; moving; romantic

That's what we're really talking about here.
The definition in my mouth. Tongue the words[14] into meat words make me meat. Make me sweet. The definition in yr mouth. One type[15]

making. I prefer to find out on my
hands & knees how to make us

the guttural

---

14. See programming

15. Re: love

CLEANLINESS IS NEXT

                              (It only gets violent when I'm in love

Consider yr focus. Consider wrd choice

                              (It only gets violent when I'm in lust

The best answer

                              (Each other on the phone. Where r u he asks. I'm good *she replies. I mean good. Good!*

The robot it corrects

The essay describes him as: 5'9" with brown eyes light brown hair like sparrow wings & small hands. He is my best friend.

The question being: so what?[16]

He is eighteen & works at the Kinko's. He drinks Brass Monkeys & is very smart with computers

(The description of his physical should give insight into

---

16. If I use a refrigerator to refrigerate it is not an object but a refrigerator and in that sense I do not possess it

Such as my beady lizard eyes & how he liked to see that hole

*(Did I ever tell you you have
beautiful eyes Daddy says*

empty. Such as the one wherein I am a song that gets stuck in yr head. Such as the one wherein the webcam makes me beautiful anime[17]. Or wherein I should cut my face[18] so I'm not so pretty

Once[19] he drew me a bath & lit candles & the roses smelled like candles

---

17. #nofilter
18. An object no longer specified by its function is defined by the subject
19. In the passionate abstractness of possession all objects are equivalent

(It doesn't have to be the truth it just has to be the right

I would not define it

(My body before i

Interests : Music : Books : School : Employment : Pics :

(t was glass

Wherein he licks my hairy
armpit					on camera[20]

										(Tongue the salt from yr upper lip

to absorb pheromones for when you tap tap
the screen		repulsed

										(Flipping right to the scratch-and-
										sniff to finger where the dog[21] gets
										skunked

---

20. Pronounced *cahm uh ruh*
21. Precisely because it sends back not real images, but desired ones

Baked Alaska among other things has a time & a place. This way we understand each other

(I ask is there a difference between knowledge & information

The process is arduous. No matter how many times I read the paragraph I still don't know what I am. This is not the case for euphemism

(I know how I like it & you're doing it intimacy

As defined by.[22] The act[23] brings into existence

(Search

---

22. General knowledge need not be cited
23. Something that somebody

engine

The results are what was meant.
If you type *how to*

        love lyrics   tie a tie   love lil wayne

Level emote. Not the mechanical although the robot voice is kind of sweet. Not the internal[24]. Biology & no two cunts look the same. The internal[25] like a red red rose. Like the coloring book on my coffee table.[26] The fire at the end of flambé. Everyone knows what it feels like
this lov   emaking

(I typed butt plugs & he said lol

Without cadence
smells like   like   like it's   like

---

24. Is a specialized fluid composed mainly of erythrocytes, leukocytes and platelets suspended in a liquid called plasma. In vertebrates it is bright red when

25. Domesticate

26. VULVES A COLORIER; EL LIBRO PARA COLOREAR DE "COÑO"; MÖSENMALBUCH

THE SCORES ARE CURVED

For example biology again. Biology brings into existence but biology is not lovemaking. Biology is intercourse[27]. Biology is babies & stick-y-outty stick-y-inny.　　　　Yr this & this. His that that.
　　Not I

like my hair this way

　　　　　　　　　　　　(Is it wrong for women to wear the
　　　　　　　　　　　　tie of the oppressor

---

27. Sex

Something about how we're all human. Something about the necessity of putting the square peg in the square hole & sometimes other holes too.[28]

What grows between us & it's pretty & hard but also delicate & it feels delicate[29]. Say lovemaking the definitive

                              (My body's relation[30] ship to itself

I don't know what I'm building

---

28. In Anne Sexton's poem, "The Kiss," for example, when she writes *Once it was a boat, quite wooden/and with no business, no salt water under it/and in need of some paint* she is referring to

29. Afraid of what my own voice

30. "greater than" or "less than"

But I'm[31]
built on.   Correct or ~~correcting~~

(Like the cops he says. No visible

The mark[32]

(Red pen

Lovemaking marked[33]

(When they cut open their heads after death there was no difference between woman & shemale the feminine

A maker[34]

---

31. The three-paragraph essay, in fact
32. A target or something somebody aims at with
33. Desired or required standard
34. Little red flags tied so you don't lose

YR WAY

In the box there is a bar of soap. In the bar of soap there is a woman. This is called tradition. In every American there is a shelf. On the shelf is a box & in that box is a bar of soap. Named it Television as if it were just a box with a mirror. Soft brown soap tallow or green spring the ivory body wash in a box on a shelf exactly where we left it. Thank God you have it too. This is evolution. Most importantly the bar of soap is a bar of soap. Let me show you everything origin. She is wearing yellow rubber gloves

(If humans were animals we wouldn't have the word animals

In another box sleeps it. Hairy perfumed strumpet. That is the real objective. Or in any other name: he/she/a rose/

(In his anger he looks upon the basketball team & cannot tell which women would suck his

continuity[35]. In the commercial there is a bar of soap. In the bar of soap there is a woman. Minus her face[36]. In the commercial there is a woman. This is just how things are

---

35. Taken or used forcefully or without permission
36. Especially in a challenge, and usually with hostility, criticism or defiance

Ideas for Classification & Division:

> "Have you ever encountered a stereotype—a statement that treats a wide variety of individuals as if they were all alike? You may have heard, for example, that all New Yorkers are rude, all Westerners love the great outdoors, all Newfoundlanders tell funny stories. If you happen to be from any of these places, you know for a fact that a group of people   often reduced   & write an
>   individual within"

(Award-winning Chicana lesbian feminist writer & prolific editor who likes to take it up the

But I know everything is in a person's shoes. Let's make love making various. Sweet innocent & her high school boyfriend

(The term is Italian Virgin. In other words a nice Catholic girl who loves her boyfriend & God's loop

holes

In the box is a bar of soap. In the bar of soap is a woman. In the woman is a silence. This is not[37]. Inside this silence. The way out. Now the box is the size of a room. Now the box is the size of a door. Now the box is the size of yr folded palms. You can't remember the word for it

---

37. Before the words comes an image. At a molecular level the color blue is the body's

(animal

SITUATION (ELLE)

Hey little girl[38]
everyone sees you. My sweet little girl[39]

Who wants a little girl[40]
on girl

Action denied. Little girls who have a reaction to [   ]. Cross out
little girls who have potential to [   ].
Little girl[41]

[   ]

[   ]

[   ]

---

38. Female child; young woman; woman of any age
39. Daughter; girlfriend; way of addressing woman
40. Offensive term; female animal
41. Maiden; damsel; lass; maid; and/or potentially a reaction to the aforementioned

[   ]
[   ]
[   ]
[   ]
[   ]
[   ]
[   ]
[   ][42]

---

42. Given the context

WILL THE LANGUAGE

Here[43] like here. Like oven like crawlspace like gum wrapper. You lean back in the chair feet on the rail

*(I just take myself everywhere I go
w/ cowboy boots*

Natural

protection : the one thing can't remove : natural body[44] : the subjective : I want to take you everywhere I

(Looking for collapse

---

43. In, at or to this place or position. In the immediate vicinity, the area one is inhabiting, proximal. I.e. This place
44. The main or central part

On the bed is a silver watch. On the screen is a gold watch. If you touch the gold watch you will receive a shock. If you touch the silver watch it is yrs. Painfully[45] the gold watch is more valuable

>   *(I am so trapped in bars of*
>   *childhood[46]*

You come over & we make tea. Look we both like Earl Grey! You are say what I say. This happiness

>   *(I learned[47] how to avoid regular*
>   *rhythm &*

I tell you the gold watch is yrs. You will never forget my blue bedspread. In the shock I am & it makes you. Wet yr fingers return to the tender spot

---

45. Having actual physical existence
46. A pattern learned by rote
47. Existing as a product of dreams or the imagination

Since when is YOU not inherent to THERE[48]? *X marks the spot they say. Please stand on yr own X*

SHE minus a small letter: HE

In the discourse discourse. *Language they say brings us together*

The words are paramount[49]

---

48. In, at or to that place or position. At some distance from the [   ], non-proximal. I.e. That place
49. To straddle

In other words: HERE: sewn to heels of I with red thread
In other words: SHE/HE/you are THERE
In other words: when you say you are HERE
      at what point the conversion?

(Closed in the hand[50]. Jinx you owe me. A beer.   Leads to another

In other words : touch is never isolate[51]: we rub off on   like
           butterfly wings

---

50. The end part of a forelimb; a bunch of bananas; a pledge of marriage
51. To hold gently between the tongue and the roof of your mouth

An argument for the stability of orgasms:

Real careen. Real pinched. Or safe[52] in the floral box. If you have never broken a bone you are an imitation

As soon as we are born into loss. No one who lived past thirty. I say find the blue fish & you point to my chest

I am a[53] person. I wear ripped T-shirts. I like violins in rock songs. I listen to NPR & don't eat cows. I drink whisky neat. Find yr own drink

In that moment a huge [   ]. All I want is what you want which is whisky neat. To [   ] you on my fingers all day. In that moment the [   ] of light. Purely [   ]. There is no metaphor during

---

52. Having no substance, reality or existence
53. Genuine and original, and so not artificial or synthetic

The thin line between so I open[54] over & over

                                                (Inside part   ed

So myself over & over. This body[55]. I don't remember going under

                                                (Minus the body I cannot even
                                              pretend

I don't remember the do
                      or[56]

---

54. Independently of the individual mind or perception
55. In a position allowing access
56. A poetic word used to introduce a rephrasing synonym or correction of a statement just made

This is the you of poetry[57]. Cut into a string of paper dolls. This is the object[58]. In the language I slide you the scalpel from inside.

In the skin a great sticky silence. Skin in skin. Everything I say stacked up in the space. Protrude[59] against me. Three years later we fall into bed in the same fantastic order. Hence in the muscle here become   double come

split

Also on the palms

---

57. All the galaxies that are known or thought to exist in space
58. Especially the complete work of a single artist
59. For space exists only when it is opened up, animated, invested with rhythm and expanded by correlation

You have said differentiate[60]. You are you. I am not you. On my paper : in truth[61]

(I

---

60. THERE fracture subject into objects
61. I

Questions consist of a collection of pairs. You must circle the one which is more likely real

(Something good happened/Some thing bad happened

Yr fingers return to the

62

62. Tender

DOPPELGANGER(S)

My problem then its twoness

(The body / the body / ten thousand thing.[63] The brain / the heart. The heart / the hand. The handhold /

In the air bird is bird. Also a soul at times. We still draw tiny brushed arc.   Does it matter[64]

---

63. Remember: the small letter: (S)HE
64. Unable to penetrate

You the you of poetry[65]. Impossible to pin to the wallpaper. As I write these words

(When you learn something it becomes a part of yr

Better half

---

65. A body

I got lost somewhere out west   fractured audience

I got lost split west

SHE the point horizon

If HE wasn't driving I'd never return[66]

---

66. Consider replacing all HE with SHE and vice versa

I looking out at the pretty girls at 13 never once feeling how boy's body could I posed naked in the mirror like *Playboy* I was like 5 when I started to masturbate again I had a penis up in front of the class & everyone was staring I chased the boys at recess & tried to kiss them

(The child's name is Storm. The child is being raised in a gender-neutral[67] environment. It is a social   experiment

coalescing
around yr   magic   markers

---

67. With zero electric charge or potential

After HE is gone I see you
everywhere. A sock
in my pants.[68] This lipstick
conundrum

                          (After image[69]. The way our voices
                          sound the same on the phone

In the hand bird is. Yr screen
shot inherently female

                          (Not only do I like to be fucked in the
                          ass but you do[70]

Etc.
Etc.

---

68. Or we may say that the mirror is a symbolic object which not only reflects the characteristics of the individual but also echoes in its expansion the historical expansion of individual consciousness

69. To walk around like someone with long hair

70. Too

Relative ly

> *(I wake up every couple of days &*
> *realize in my dream I was a boy.*
> *Little curly blond the constant shift*
> *ing from 1st to 3rd person as if to*
> *disembody*

Really just HERE v. THERE & the you that is not you who is me now. Driving east

> *(Everything that is possible is*
> *taxonomy*

A wall. One of those invisible ones the kind with the little bell you keep ringing by accident

Both you & you & you

He tells me gender is always conflated with sex

(That's the point honey

My mother chose a boy's name but not a girl's afraid to jinx me. What would she do with a boy? she asks me. I am twelve. What would she do with a boy?

I'm surprised she says. *Not very surprised but surprised*

I just want things to be easy for you she says

You look better in pants don't you he says

[Rules for the affair]

He can only get handjobs

She can only get handjobs

Lol she says. That's a good one

No mouth on genital / genital on genital / no internal stimulation

Lol she says

This is not about the body this is about rights treatment or value equal the natural give &

She has one more hole than the rules cover

He campaigns. A platform of sameness

Lol she says

What the fuck a handjob he says

Exactly

WHEN YOU LEARN SOMETHING IT BECOMES A PART OF YOUR BODY

Penis[71]   Vagina[72]

Penis[73]   Vagina[74]

Penis[75]   Vagina[76]

---

71. Pendant. Pencil in. Penetrate
72. Vaccinations. Vacillating. Vacillate
73. Penetrated. Penetratingly. Penetration
74. Vacuity. Vagrants. Vague
75. Pennant. Penitent. Penniless
76. Vain. Vainglorious. Valediction

HOW TO SET

Point at the sky. I say blue & you say blue. This is conditioning this is not blue. The smallest distance between peaks

(They say the crime rate goes up in summer because more people

Walk outside. Tell me the name of that tree tell me the feature[77]. What have you named lately? What uncomfortable seat

(When the tree falls. The bird in the tree the bright flapping. The bird in the hand[78]

---

77. Familiar landmark: nose; mouth; stubble; upper arms
78. A degree of closeness to the actual involvement

Reasons why everything must exist in place:

Action & reaction

The rules of narrative

We spent the whole movie trying to figure out what city it was supposed to be. Finally we settled on Baltimore

The yellow cat asleep on the kitchen table in a square of yellow sunlight

Alone I lose the shape of my body

A number of unidentified stains on my new pants

There are actual studies now that prove language shapes our perception of reality

The signifying hoodie

I've slept with so many people[79]

(The X is on the body

Every time we touch each other. This is the literal meaning. Location. Home. Status. Cause to be in. This is no longer. No loiter. You can't stay here. The lens. Telescoping distances they

(X

They

(X

They

(X

They

---

79. And/or

*(For 5 mths we tried to make it work.
I took pictures with 1 2 3 fingers in
my pussy they're still saved in a
folder called*

Walk outside. Describe where you are. Past tense is standard

Forces acting on a body

Attic v. basement

"How can I be racist? I don't even know any black people."

How the space you grow up in structures yr dreams

When he says "obviously you're not from here"

Did you know parts of Gotham City are located in New Jersey

Did you know even poets make art[80]

---

80. The tensions between direction and

W/o street signs. Time to turn. The voice is feminine & vaguely British. Landmarks scoured. Watch the scenery go by like beautifully constructed scenery. W/o intent

(Ap

propriate

walk outside. You are naked. There is no other way to remember. Even the blind[81]. What other options. The bird in the hand. The bird inserted

---

81. A plant in which growth stops because the growing point is damaged

Exhibit screen uni
verse. We cannot even see another
blue. Everything must exist[82]. In place. Therefore
place must exist[83]. Our human growth
spot. In place. Augmented
reality. The uncanny
valley

*("At least over there he loves me
enough to stab me")*

---

82. The ability to hold two opposing ideas in the mind

83. Whether as packaging, window or partition, glass is the basis of a transparency without transition: we see, but cannot touch

CONTINUE (UM)

Looking for the perfect haircut

> *(If you were an animal[84] which animal would you*

Mate. Reproduce. Pair off. Our system elaborates. Those silly birds of paradise. The female is always unre

markable

> *(Based entirely on the style of yr shoes*

---

84. Remembering the ugly duckling is in fact male

When I thought no difference between men & women

                                        (The holes misaligned

A small hard wrinkled seed with one green eye

A band like thin rubber pink but not: stretch & release. Tug & release. Also the faint scent of steam

                                        (If only we didn't try to be bigger than our hearts with our hearts. If only we never moved & had no need for boxes

I have always thought that if something can be imagined

(People really do look just like their pets

Plan: get rid of all my dresses

Plan: shaved head

Plan: wear nothing but dresses

Plan: or buy a tie

(Women's pants are weird

Plan: the variety of nubbins & anti-nubbins

Plan: the scientific method[85]

(as blow-up sex-sheep

---

85. A "fair test" occurs when you change only one variable and keep all other conditions the same

If you were an animal. In a fantasy world of furry holes & sticks. The species is prehensile

(Like on a continuum from male to

Peacock one day boa the next. Unicorn v. dragon.[86] We are essentially

(gay: a clear argument[87] for bestiality

---

86. Westerners understand the "magic" but not the "realism"
87. Because metaphor is

"For instance, Vagina/Penis on page 2. That seems too obvious. You've just talked about anal sex & crotch stuffing. Anyone who's fucked men & women knows the biggest physical differences are the face stubble & the arms"

There is also an argument for love & sex with robots[88]

(How we have meaningful relationships with our pets[89]

---

88. *Love + Sex with Robots.* David Levy (2007 Harper Collins)
89. For all its humanness, it always remains quite visibly an object, and hence

Our nouns are so not gendered like

(She said she'd be a jellyfish & I was jealous I didn't come up with something equally

evolved

EPILOGUE: THE GOOD GUIDE

Have dinner ready. Plan ahead, even the night before to have a delicious meal ready on time for her[90] return. This is a way of letting her[91] know that you are thinking about her[92] and are concerned about her[93] needs

Prepare for her[94]. Take 15 minutes to rest so you are refreshed when she[95] arrives. Touch up make-up put a ribbon in your hair and be fresh-looking

---

90. From the original: his
91. Him
92. Him
93. His
94. Him
95. He

Clear away the clutter[96]. Make one last trip through the main part of the house just before she[97] arrives

Over the cooler months of the year you should light a fire for her[98] to unwind by. She[99] will feel she[100] has reached a haven of rest and order and this will give you a lift too. After all catering for her[101] comfort will provide you with immense personal[102] satisfaction

---

96. Classification of nouns and pronouns in certain languages according to the forms taken by adjectives, modifiers and other grammatical items associated syntactically

97. He

98. Him

99. He

100. He

101. His

102. And/or political

Prepare the children. Take a few minutes to wash the children's hands and faces (if they are small) comb their hair and if necessary change their clothes. They are little treasures and she[103] would like to see them playing the part. Minimize all noise. At the time of her[104] arrival eliminate all noise of the washer dryer or vacuum. Try to encourage the children to be quiet

Be happy to see her[105]

Greet her[106] with a warm smile and show sincerity in your desire[107] to please

---

103. He
104. His
105. Him
106. Him
107. Is the opposite of

Listen to her[108]. You may have a dozen important things to tell her[109] but the moment of arrival is not the time. Let her[110] talk first – remember her[111] topics of conversation are more important than yours

---

108. Him
109. Him
110. Him
111. His

Make the evening hers[112]. Never complain if she[113] comes home late or goes out to dinner or other places of entertainment without you. Instead try to understand her[114] world of strain and pressure and very real need to be at home and relax

Your goal: Try to make sure home is a place of peace order and tranquility where she[115] can renew in body and

---

112. His
113. He
114. His
115. He

Don't greet her[116] with complaints and problems

Don't complain if she[117]'s home late for dinner or even if she[118] stays out all night. Count this as minor compared to what she[119] might have gone through that day

---

116. Him
117. He
118. He
119. He

Make her[120] comfortable. Have her[121] lean back in a comfortable chair or have her[122] lie down in the bedroom. Have a cool or warm drink ready for her[123]

Arrange her[124] pillow and offer to take off her[125] shoes. Speak in a low soothing and pleasant voice

Don't ask her[126] questions about her[127] actions or question her[128] judgment or integrity. Remember she[129] is the master of the house and as such she[130] will always exercise her[131] will with fairness and truthfulness. You have no right to question her[132]

---

120. Him
121. Him
122. Him
123. Him
124. His
125. His
126. Him
127. His
128. His
129. He
130. He
131. His
132. Him

Be a little gay and a little more interesting

ACKNOWLEDGEMENTS

Earlier versions of "WILL THE LANGUAGE", "DOPPELGANGER(S)", "HOW TO SET" and "CONTINUE (UM)" were published in the chapbook *OBJECT REFERENCE NOT SET TO AN INSTANCE OF OBJECT* (dancing girl press). Huge thanks to Kristy Bowen and dancing girl press for supporting this project along the way.

Earlier versions of "DEFINITION THE BODY", "CLEANLINESS IS NEXT", and "THE SCORES ARE CURVED" appeared in > *kill author*, and a version of "WHEN YOU LEARN SOMETHING IT BECOMES A PART OF YOUR BODY" was published in the *FUCK POEMS* anthology edited by Vincent Cellucci (Lavender Ink). Again, big thanks, and a lotta <3, Vince.

The entire text, excepting the footnoting/pronouns, of "THE GOOD GUIDE" was taken from "The Good Wife's Guide," supposedly published in a magazine or home economics text book in the 1950s, but the real origin of which has not been confirmed. The author discovered a copy of it stuck under the windshield wiper of her car.

This work also refers to or makes use of ideas and language from various places, including news articles, composition writing exercises, writer bios, the *Tao De Jing*, autocorrect, and the Microsoft Word thesaurus, and from various people, including Anne Sexton, Ariana Reines, Jean Baudrillard (*The System of Objects*) and Dewitt Brinson. If you, too, think you recognize your words in here, you probably do. Thank you all for your beautiful, interesting, weird words.

The author would like to express endless gratitude for her LSU and New Orleans families—with particular thanks to Moira Crone, Rodger Kamenetz, Laura Mullen, the Manatees and the New Orleans Poetry Brothel—for their epic support and inspiration. And for setting the bar so high.

Thank you to Mel Coyle for keeping my glass half and/or full.

Thank you to my parents, Thomas Nunes and Stacie Nunes, for always managing to be "surprised, but not too surprised." So. Much. Love.

And, of course, many many many thanks to Dawn Lundy Martin and to Switchback Books, who so warmly welcomed me into the family and gave this work a home.

Jenn Marie Nunes is the author of four chapbooks, including the collaborative *OPERA TRANS OPERA* (alice blue books), and is co-founding editor of *TENDE RLOIN*, an online gallery for poetry. She lives in New Orleans "with her girlfriend and her dog."